The Guide to Being Black in IT

How I Made It in IT Without a Degree and How You Can Do the Same

D.A Pearson

Dedication Page

This is dedicated to all the black men and women attempting to get into the world of Information Technology and wealth building. I dedicate this piece of work to the poor, the middle class, and the unemployed—to that lost ship sailing into the dark and unsettling abyss of hard grind and faith. I was once a lost ship too, but I found navigation. I just want to share my map with you.

Contents

Acknowledgements

Preface

Part One: My Story

Turning Tech

Part Two: Your Guide to the IT Game

Should I Go To College?
Getting Started
Know Your Goals and Values
Contracting
Understand Job Descriptions
Interview with Confidence
Know Your Monetary Worth
Learn How to Negotiate
Be Smart With Your Money
Networking
Schmooze 'Em
References
Coworkers
Shake Them Haters Off
Harassment at Work
Put Your Health First
Software and Technology Recommendations
Certifications

A Perfect World Plan

Conclusion

About the Author

Acknowledgements

I want to give a special thank you to everyone who has inspired and supported me at some point:

Debra Pearson
My beautiful wife, Kesh
My grandma, Nanny
Brent Pearson
My editor, Ren Jones
Masai Polk
Aunti Di and Uncle Barry
Uncle Billy
Stakk Doe
Brother Carl and the nation
Josh G
Mic Titan
Coach
Yay yizz
Big LT
EB
D.O. Double-LA
Finchiavill Films
International Yusuf
Melody Waters
Mr. Roddy
Tyrick
Mr. Maklad
Scott Atkinson
Tony Williamette

Dr. Umar
Dr. Boyce Watkins
Dr. Claude Anderson
TNT Barbershop
Century College
South High
Urban League
Mpls Park Board
Microsoft
Clubflyers
Upwork
Hip Hop, all forms
Southside Mpls
Southeast Mpls
Eastside St Paul
Frogtown
Northside Mpls

Thank you for being a part of my journey.

Preface

From the bottom of my heart, thank you for investing in and supporting me and my novel. I published this book in order to tell my story—the story of a black man who raised himself out of poverty without obtaining a college degree and who forced his way into the IT industry where black people are still a minority. I want to share how I have made all of my dreams come true in a world that tried to keep me down, while also providing a guide for other black men and women to do the same.

I wrote this novel explicitly, unapologetically, and directly for my black brothers and sisters to show you my stumbles and blunders as well as my triumphs. As technology evolves and gains tighter control of humanity, we must find a way to benefit from technology without allowing ourselves to become entrapped in student loan debt and predatory lending. We must find a way to thrive and build economic think tanks and businesses that allow money to flourish in our communities. We must find ways to become subject matter experts on the new and forthcoming technology so that we can obtain a technical and financial advantage in this technology-driven society.

We will cover the pitfalls and dark corners of the IT industry and how to navigate around them to your advantage. We will go through real stories that I have witnessed and been a part of (though the names have been changed for anonymity), and I will approach each situation with brutal honesty. I came into this universe with the gift and curse to tell it like it is, and I want to use that honesty to open up a conversation about how we have to handle ourselves and others in business and how to maintain a clear mind when making these decisions.

This novel is only half of the conversation—as you read this book, document your comments, compliments, disagreements, and questions, and email them to me. Let's turn this story into a dialogue.

D.A. Pearson

Part 1: My Story

In all honesty, my dream was never to be in IT. I wanted to be the first black entomologist on National Geographic. As you can imagine, not too many blacks were interested in studying insects at that time. My interest lasted until I was about 10 years old—once I learned the world of monto blocks, blades, Cutlasses, and Chevy Caprices. I was raised in the streets when it comes to hustling and influences, after all, and these were the things I wanted to have—things I thought I needed to have. I didn't know how I was going to get them, but I guess I thought entomology was not going to be it.

I always wanted to grow up like the Cosby's, but I related more to Good Times. I didn't know anyone who lived like the Huxtables, and we didn't see doctors and lawyers that looked like us (even though the U of M was only two blocks away). Everyone I knew lived similar to Good Times. I didn't even realize we were poor until I was in the lunch line one day, holding a sheet that had my house's annual income listed on it. The lunch lady looked at the sheet sadly and then asked me how do we survive. I was embarrassed. Eventually kids started saying my family was on food stamps and that their dad paid for us with his taxes. We had food every day and gifts during Christmas, so I didn't know the difference. I should have told those kids that their dad may have paid his taxes, but his ancestors have a debt to my ancestors that they never paid back.

I never had much guidance figuring out what I was going to do with my life. Neither of my parents had degrees. My mom took a couple college courses, and my pops only had an 8th grade education. He also left when I was about 13. My mom did the best that she could to raise a young black man on her own, but there was only so much she could do with little income, especially after she got sick. But she gave me everything I needed—life, morals, and values. It was my job to figure out the rest, and I refused to play the victim.

My humble and self-propelled life in the IT world started around 1996 when my mom sent me upstairs to get something off the top shelf in her closet. She was going to the MN school of business at the time, and when I reached up to the closet shelf, an old computer support book fell on my foot. It was so heavy and hurt so bad that I just knew it had some good info. An hour later, I heard a shout from downstairs from my mom wondering where the hell I was with her requested item. I was curled up in her closet on chapter 5. I learned the inside components of a desktop within an hour, and it completely changed my life.

After my painful introduction to computers, I went to various computer shops and asked for old parts that they did not want. I was always told no. So eventually, I found a large backpack, attached a cart to my bike, casually walked to the dumpsters in the alley, and took the old computers and parts out of the trash. Tip: Refuse to take no for an answer.

I went and got a job at Cub Foods and would take the 16 to General Nanosystems to buy parts, piece by piece, to build my own computer system. I kept learning about computers and kept my interest in them, but I didn't consider it a career. I was still trying to figure out how I was going to make it in the world and, at the time, I was husting—the semi-legal kind.

I took a few classes at IPR and learned how to mix records, and I thought I was the shit. In hindsight, I sucked. Real bad. But I was really dedicated to making music. I specifically remember trudging through the snow with one of my Southeast Mpls buddies to record. Times had gotten hard and he had sold his box Chevy, so we took the 16 bus and walked the rest of the way down to Washington Avenue. We were determined.

I even bought an MPC 2000 (you know, the machine that you tap buttons on to make your own beats) to make beats through influences of Pete Rock, DJ Premier, and Juicy J. My homeboy Ern sold it to me on consignment. I didn't have all of the money, so I said "let me get that, make some money, and then pay you the rest." I had already bought a duplicator from him, so he figured I was good for it. I kept my word and paid him back in full within two payments.

Me and my team kept making music, and we started selling mixtapes in the hood. We did this full time for a while, but I realized that I needed real money. I figured I could always make music, but I needed to get some bread. What I didn't realize was that I was still learning more about IT by making music; I was using computers to engineer beats, and I was the best at IPR for the PC/Mac class.

Some of my friends had all the spoils of hustling—the fully-illegal kind. I saw them with all the nice cars and women, and I can't lie, I was intrigued. One of my friends had a grey caprice coupe with TV's in it and a nice sound system. It was very clean, and damn I wanted it. Then the day came when he was going to sell it, and I didn't have the money to buy it. I was upset—not at him, but because I didn't know how to quickly obtain that kind of cash. And he only wanted $1,000. He had plans of throwing blades on it, but he didn't do it. But he did go through two paint jobs that were painted by a dope fiend they called Paint Man who knew how to cut paint like butter on an IHOP pancake.

My dad had called my mom after a conversation we had, and he said, "Derek sounds street!" My mom told him, annoyed, "He is in the streets all the time, what do you expect?" My dad could recognize the street in me because he dealt with nothing but street people. They were all hustlers, cons, and connivers. He was from Chicago too, by way of Mississippi, so I am sure he likely had his share of street slicking. Every man I met that he hung with always had something up their sleeve. One guy we knew would scope out the dope boys. He would watch them all night, find their stash, and steal the bricks. Then he would serve them all profit. Pops didn't know I knew.

My parents had no clue that I was associated with people that were really out there in the streets. They were my friends, but I wasn't involved in any of that. I may have been in the streets, but I am blessed to say that I never cheated or robbed anyone. And when guys were chopping up dope, I would ask "how much time you get for that? How much time for this?" I wrote down the jail time you would get for the amounts on the scale, and it just did not add up for me. I figured that the time you would get for drugs would end up with you working for minimum wage. On top of that, if I ever got too interested, there was always some older dude around to tell me that "it ain't worth it" and that I was "too smart to deal." One day, my homie was chopping up and I was writing raps. His cousin came in with a shoebox of dope. I couldn't help but think that I could make a lot of money, but I knew it wasn't a good idea. I did offer to help him chop it, but he said "it makes your fingers numb," and I wasn't too interested in that. So, I just kept writing the raps.

These dudes I was around had all already been through the system and knew there were no other options for them as far as they were concerned. They'd rather me sell cd's and computers then end up in jail or on the news. I used to fix this guy's computer who had the big weed plug and wanted me to set up his home network. His fridge was full of pounds. His foreign was always clean, and he had two spots. But he was a solid guy. He always encouraged me to keep hustling and never stop.

One of my friend's brothers got shot a few blocks away from where we were hustling at. Another two guys that I knew from school got killed, another got shot, and this girl I knew got shot too. She used to braid my hair when I had cornrows. Another girl I used to visit told me to stay home one night because a war had gotten out of hand. It seemed like every time I went to go hang out with some lady, I ended up in a situation. I was often questioned about the nature of my appearance in that hood. We hustled in areas where wars were occurring, so even though we weren't affiliated, we were associated to people affiliated, and that almost made us affiliated by default. Who you know could get you killed. Affiliated or not, bullets have no names, and the streets are not safe for anyone. I saw dope spots. Dope fiends. Dope boys and dope girls. In the hood, the underworld is right out in the open. I could not help but to have a taste, but drugs and I did not mix well and all my friends knew it. My mother made it clear that if I ever got involved in "gang shit" that it was self-genocide and that I would be left to rot in jail on my own—she would not support me in any dealings or associations with people involved in street life.

I never considered myself a street guy, but I knew that I would never turn over on anyone if I had ever had a run in with the law. One of my homies used to hang with this guy. Every time this guy got jammed up by the law, he would use my homie's name and license number. I tried to convince my buddy that this guy was acting like a rat. He was upset about him using his name, but he wouldn't hear what I was saying. How could a man use another man's name for a crime that he committed and still be able to look himself in the mirror? This coward used my friend's name multiple times. I was pissed. I kept telling him this guy was going to be an informant one day, but no one believed me. Well, eventually this dude ended up telling on a bunch of guys in a federal indictment in the city. He took a 5K1 agreement against his brothers that kept money in his pocket and walked away scot-free. To this day, that man is out free while everyone else in that case has a life sentence.

Although there are a lot of shady guys out there, I also met a lot of interesting guys in the street that taught me about black diversity and who offered words of wisdom and encouragement. There was this old Elk Rukn guy, and I used to fix his computer and make mixtapes for him. He admired my hustle, and he told me, "man, you gone be rich one day." And one of the older guys (who I specifically remember had a Benz truck) even told me that I should open a shop, though I didn't see the vision until years later once I had built up confidence in my skills.

One guy who inspired me had started his own trucking company in the South. He went down to Atlanta, saw what black folks were doing down there, and took his grind to the next level. Never believe what the media tells you about young black men! Brothers down there have hustle like no other, and street guys know how to turn it around.

My mom was a professional who worked for the U of M in administrative positions. Through her, I got my typing and soft skills. My pops was a hustler; he would sell stuff, paint, work on cars, and do any other job because he was a good talker. So, I got all of those skills from him. Degree or not, I figured out a way to propel myself into success using what I had. I figured out how to get comfortable with being uncomfortable and how to get out of my comfort zone to make it work.

Turning Tech

One hot summer day in 2003, I went up to CompUSA in Roseville (which is now closed) to buy a CD burner or some other kind of computer part. As soon as I walked in the front doors, I saw a sign: Now hiring computer support specialists. I walked up to the front desk and told the nearest employee that I wanted to apply. He flatly responded with "you need an A+ certification." Mind you, he never even asked about my qualifications or experience—he just assumed because I was black that I couldn't possibly have an A+ certification. I mean, I didn't have an A+ certification, but I had been building my own computers and helping my neighbors with any tech work they needed. After hearing this new information, the guy said that I would never be able to work there with that, and he rudely walked away. I never did work at that CompUSA, but let the record reflect that they are out of business.

After leaving CompUSA, I immediately went home and ordered some business cards from Vistaprint. Having someone tell me it wouldn't work was like someone challenging me to make it work my damn self. When my business cards came in, I started passing them out in the hood. I didn't know how I was going to make it work, but I knew three things were not an option for me: selling dope, playing in the NBA, or working a dead end job. So, I had to find something else to do, and information technology was going to be my way out. (Interestingly enough, I had been in the IT game for several years before I even called it IT. I don't think I used that word until 2014.)

So, I was passing out business cards, but I was not getting many calls. Computer support was still new to my peers. I took a dead end job at the Frogtown Sears in 2006 to set me straight. I was living in the projects on 6th and Cedar, in Cedar Square West. I admit I had gotten content with the life of Hennessy and mixtapes that I was living. But that life started to eat away at my spirit. One night, I downed about 7 shots and ended up reading the entire book of Revelations. When I woke up the next morning, I was determined to make a change. I needed to grow, and I had to change my way of thinking. I realized that the route I was taking didn't make sense. Street hustling, for me, was dead.

I kept my merch support job at Sears for a few months and hated it, but I was determined to move into a new apartment. I moved over to Lake Street at the beginning of 2007 and enrolled in an A+ course on the northside at the Urban League. The Urban League taught me a lot about applications, Avast antivirus, and many other things. There were some good brothers in that program, and one of them, Rob, designed my first support flyer.

Our teacher at the Urban League was named Adria. I use some

of the same tools and tactics that she used then in the classes I instruct now. She made me a better IT professional. Thanks to her teachings, I ended up landing an internship at a non-profit called Urban Ventures that same year. I got this connection through one of the brothers at MAD DADS. At that point, I was doing computer repair at one of my buddy's shops, and we had a 50/50 agreement on the rent. Things were going slow for me, and then I got a random call inviting me to come down to 4th Avenue for an interview at Urban Ventures. I had been working on computers all day, and I was filthy. I told the manager that I was not ready for an interview with my attire. He said come anyway.

When I arrived, the interview went like this:

Manager
Do you have experience in hardware?

Me
Yes, I built my own computer and installed drives.

Manager
What do you know about Windows?

Me
I have installed Windows 98 and XP.

Manager
Have you installed any operating systems?

Me

I do OS wipes on the regular.

I was hired within 20 minutes. And just like that, in mid-2007, my career really took off.

The Cristo Rey Jesuit High School/Colin Powell Center was my first big project. We installed desktops and supported teachers, executives, and the Urban Venture staff. I learned how to image laptops and desktops with Norton ghost, supported Server 2003 by resetting passwords, supported Apple Macs, helped a network vendor install network switches, installed VoIP phones, managed Cisco admin consoles, worked in the domain, and migrated users from Outlook 2003 to Outlook 2007. This internship was equivalent to a two-year degree. I was paid $10 per hour and only had a short bus ride commute. My supervisor told me, "Derek, you will never make $10 per hour again." He was right. I never did!

Side note: I recently said those same words to one of my students. He landed a contract with Allina supporting Epic and Mychart. This guy was a security officer, and he landed an IT job that has the potential to go permanent after one year at $50-60K, all within 1 month of completing my MTA class (I'm a bad man!).

In the tech industry, it is incredibly important that you stay up-to-date with changes in technology. So, in November 2016, I read the book for the Microsoft Certification test in two weeks and passed the exam.

I bought a Chevy Lumina, and the transmission went out in 2 weeks. I got back on the bus and upped my hustle. In 2008, I started charging people $75 to wipe their PCs. I saved up $1,500 in two weeks and bought a Dodge Spirit. I also found a plug for desktops in Hammond, Indiana that sold me desktops for $250. I bought them, installed Windows XP on them, loaded the drivers, and sold them for $350-400. All shipping was free, and I had all profit.

I sold my first PC to a guy named Big Rob. He needed a desktop, and I promised to support it if he had any problems. All of my business was completed with hand shake deals. The streets had taught me to honor word over paperwork because we never trusted corporate-type dealings. In the corporate world, even papers can lie. I didn't need documents to help me keep my word.

After July 2008, I landed a four month contract through Robert Half at Coloplast Corp to do desktop support.

There I was making $16 per hour. In corporate America. Still no degree.

The week before the contract started with Coloplast, I was rear-ended, and my car was totaled. I started a lawsuit for the accident, drove a rental car for a few weeks, and accepted a payout for my totaled car.

After the wreck, I had a White Bonneville with leather seats that I bought from Big Rob for $400, a 1982 Buick Lesabre coupe, and my own place. When I went on dates, the women always thought I was selling, but I wasn't selling drugs—I was selling computers. That year I likely cleared $8-12K off hustling alone, not even including my actual job. Of course, all of that extra money regrettably went to unnecessary things and the fast life after work. Plus, that 82 Lesabre had a leaking gas tank that ate up a bit of money. I wondered why my gas was low most of the time (until I wised up), but I loved that car all the same, with its comfy, couch-like seats and its Pioneer system (plenty UGK, 8ball, and MJG bumped from that system). I had a guy replace the gas tank in Apple Valley, and I kept right on riding. Not even bad weather could not keep me in the house; I just had to show off my 82!

One thing about me was that I did not have patience, and I was always cautious about who I associated with. I had worked too hard to let someone else's drama come in and ruin everything I had built up for myself.

A guy dropped his laptop off to me, and I reloaded Windows on it for $100. When he came back to pick it up, he had a few staples in his head. He asked me if I wanted to hang out, and I responded by asking him what happened to his head. He said he was with some guys that got shot at by some other dudes. That was enough info for me. I figured if I hung out with him, I would end up in one of those situations too, so I told him I was just too busy. Tip: When someone shows you who they are, believe them. Don't connect with people that don't align with your vision.

The Coloplast job gave me enterprise experience. I was hired as a new hire coordinator, and my job was to set new hires up with their laptops and do some light support. I had to work with this redneck that was super prejudice. He always hated on me, but I didn't pay him much mind. I was there for the experience and the check. I got to learn Avaya phones, and I also imaged a lot of laptops.

In July 2008, I found out I had diabetes after I almost died driving to Fairview with a blood sugar of 1200. Then, towards the end of 2008 and the end of my contract, I had decided that I was tired of the corporate world, so me and my friends decided to open a shop on 34th and Minnehaha. I took my tax money and my rent money, and we all put our funds together for a commercial lease deposit. I knew that meant that I was probably going to get evicted, but I thought that it was a risk worth taking. I was willing to sleep in that 82 if it meant opening that store.

We opened the Minnehaha One Stop Shop and registered an LLC in March 2009. We were owners. For the first week, all we had for sale were mixtapes and incense. Then we ordered clothes and shoes. I need to point out the fact that black women were our biggest supporters and without them, we would never have been successful.

I started doing computer repair and computer resale in the shop, which went well and saved people money as opposed to going to corporate, name-brand tech support and getting jipped. Really, most times I was the one getting jipped when I started because people did not want to pay once they saw how fast I did the job, so I felt bad and cut them a deal. I had to stop that. As black folks, we will pay everyone and their mama, but then we want a discount any time we do business with our own people. We have to do better and start supporting each other rather than taking advantage of each other.

In March 2009, somebody crashed into my 82 Buick Lesabre coupe (yep, my baby) when I was on my way to the shop. Around this time, the settlement from my first car wreck came back. I invested $1,000 into the shop, and I bought a Dodge Stratus from a friend.

It was trash (at no fault of my friend), so I resold it to some guy in Plymouth for $900.

Then I went and got a blue 1993 Oldsmobile Delta 88. It was gorgeous. Yes, a fine fox in sheep's clothing. The sub frame fell out on me while exiting 35W at 50 mph. I ended up on the lawn of Bremer Bank with the engine 2 inches from the ground. I immediately called the seller and told him what happened, and he tried to play me to the left. So, I called my buddy Stakk Doe, and he acted like a bird-beaked lawyer named "Donald" and called the seller. The dude was terrified of a lawsuit, so he called me back and ended up giving me a raggedy ass 94 Buick Lesabre from Somerset, WI. It looked horrible. My homies roasted me for weeks. The A/C was at least freezing cold though. But I just couldn't continue to be seen in that car, so I bought a 98 Olds Regency, put in DJ Quik "Safe and Sound," and sold the raggedy 94 to this woman from the Northside.

This lady really tried to holler at me over the phone. I was trying to sell the car. She showed up to look at the car and knew it was trash, but she needed wheels and it ran like hell. She was fine, I admit, but I didn't want to mix any business with pleasure. I said, "Gimme $400, and we good". She paid, drove off, and still pursued me, but I didn't call her back (even after she left multiple voicemails). Two months later, I got a ticket and a letter in the mail saying that the car's title wasn't switched and the car was impounded. It would have been more money to get it out than what she paid me. I obviously dodged a bullet not dating that one.

My dad died in early 2009. So, I had two car accidents in a year, a near death experience from diabetes, and I lost my dad. Times had gotten tough, but I powered through it. I felt God was putting me through a test, and I refused to break. I had plans.

We started out doing $100 PC repair, but we slashed it in half to meet the needs of the residents in the area. We had a bunch of customers that always complained about getting viruses on their computers because they let their kids download and install anything. So we had a lot of return customers. Some were upset that they were having to keep getting their computers fixed, so I started making them sign contracts to make it clear that it was of no fault of ours. Then I told them to use Linux if you want to browse the bad sites. My job was not to judge. My job was to provide them with a stable operating system; so, I installed Fedora and sent them on their way. Anyone that got a Linux install from me did not have to come back. I did not make more money from the Linux installs, but I saved some customers hundreds of dollars, and that was good enough for me.

We closed the shop in March 2010. I got back into contracting and landed a job imaging computers. I worked with that company for one month before they canned me. In the end, I won a lawsuit against them. After that, I started working at an IP video surveillance company in Burnsville where I learned a lot about Apple, making $17 per hour.

That Fall, I got another settlement and blew it on cars. Looking back, I think part of the reason I bought all of those cars was because I was poor as a child and had to walk in the cold to the bus. Maybe also because a few people laughed at me walking in the cold. But the main problem was that not having a car put me at the bottom of the totem pole. And I really wasn't feeling that.

I bought all those buckets, and low and behold, I was back on the bus. God laughs at your plans. At this point, my career was not going well in Burnsville, and I was being pressured to buy a car from my supervisor.

I started doing some odd jobs and contracting here and there to make ends meet. One thing to note is that once you are in a recruiter's system for contract work, they will always have some kind of work for you if you stay in touch. So, Robert Half got me another contract, this time for a manufacturing company where I completed my first Windows 7 migration—another powerful notch to add to my resume, as companies nationwide were migrating from Windows XP to Windows 7. I also worked on smartphones for the first time, helped the company migrate from Novell to Active Directory, and got some experience supporting an ERP system. I also got something invaluable: new people in my network and good references.

My next Windows 7 migration was with Blue Cross. They had some major SCCM issues occurring, but I did well. On my very first day there, one of the systems engineers asked the team, "How many of you guys have degrees?" Almost everyone except me and a couple others raised their hands. Then he asked, "How many of you like Apple?" A few other hands raised. Then he shouted, "I don't give a damn what you know or what you think you know! We have a process here. The first person who mentions Apple is fired! We don't want to hear your suggestions!" All those guys that proudly raised their hands about their degrees were shocked. He gave them all hell, but he liked me for some reason.

A lot of people eventually got laid off, but I left before that started. I had taken a job at Traveler's Insurance, and my wife and I booked a trip to Puerto Rico. I let the background check pass while I sat on a sunny beach drinking rum. One of the Blue Cross leads left a voice message saying the project got canned. I just grinned and watched the sea crabs walk around. I knew I was headed in the right direction in my life. I thought about that jerk at CompUSA that said I would never work without an A+ certification.

At Travelers, my job was to migrate Windows XP to Windows 7. I worked 2nd shift at $25 per hour. I thought I was ballin, so I had Dante Autobody in Brooklyn Park paint my Buick 79 triple coat red. I just could not leave those Buicks alone.

Travelers gave me my SCCM experience in 2013. SCCM is basically a software suite that allows asset management, remote support, and imaging all in one package. I started teaching the other field support guys how to use it, and I gained a few friends that I still talk to now. Networking at its finest. Remember that your worth is your network. If you only know five broke people, you likely are or will be broke too.

After Travelers, I accepted a short contract for a Windows 7 role with Medica in 2014 where I used SCCM again (see how new knowledge gets you new opportunities?). After Medica, I went over to AIG and became a Windows 7 Lead. I supported all the migration roll outs for Oakdale, MN and for New York, did status reports, worked with PMs and the packaging teams, learned about maintaining spreadsheets (a valuable skill), and I did some PM and BA duties. This was my first lead experience. I got two of my friends hired on, reporting to me. One of them became an SCCM tech and another is now working as a Level 2 Engineer for Bailiwick. (The latter also knows one of my previous students who was also hired at Bailiwick. Isn't life crazy?)

That team lead position was a turning point for my career. But then my mom died in November 2014, and I could not really have given a shit about IT or anything else for that matter. I was cold and lost. All the prejudice in Minnesota finally got to me, and I was suddenly bitter. I had zero tolerance for any form of disrespect whether it was in the streets or in the workplace. Grief can dramatically affect your life and your career, and unfortunately, bereavement is not offered to contractors.

After I got myself halfway back together from my mom's death, I worked on a Commvault Project with TCS in August 2015. I was trying to heal from mom's death, and I just needed a job that was laid back. I would go to Missouri and Iowa to help cisco engineers reroute their network. I would fly in to Des Moines and Columbia, and then drive out to these backwood hick towns, tether my phone, connect the serial cord from my laptop to the router, and open Putty. 15 minutes later, the job was done. It was one of the best experiences I had. Outside of that, 2015 is a big blur. I don't remember much.

A phone call, again, changed my career, and that call was from my buddy International Yusuf. I met him when I started my first internship, and we had kept in contact since then. He traveled around the world working on solutions, and he was focused on getting Africans to implement and leverage technology. So, one day he called me and said, "We need someone to talk to kids for a coding program at Metro State University." I said, "Cool, sign me up."

I started as a guest speaker and built a curriculum using Microsoft Imagine Academy. My work resulted in me being awarded as the IT Professional of the year.

From there, my name started to travel, and I got to build a curriculum for another nonprofit.

I began training people for the Microsoft Technology Associate exams to help them gain foundational networking experience, and I also started using my placement skills. Two years later, I had gotten over 20 people certified and hired in enterprise IT positions.

One of my first placements was for one of my friends, and I felt really good about that one. He was working at Enterprise (the rental car service). I told him I had just received an email about a contract role with Compucom, and I knew he had some experience with Windows 10 and basic computer repair. So, I helped him upgrade his resume and sent him to the recruiter. He interviewed and got the position without a college degree! The company hired him full time 6 months later, and he is now Comptia A+ certified (which the company paid for) with 2 years of experience.

Another friend of mine paid a company $400 to edit his resume and only got few calls out of it. He used my template and got dozens of calls. He even landed a junior business analyst role at an energy company and went on to get his Master's in data science.

You see, my grind and smart work (work smarter, not harder) allowed me to use my network to support people that would have otherwise been receiving an underemployed salary. I created this service without taking a loan, just as me and my homies did not take a loan when we started Minnehaha One Stop Shop in South Mpls.

As an instructor, I make using AWS or Azure a requirement in my classes because, even though everything is headed towards the cloud, there will always be some physical hardware somewhere (which means another job for you). Remember that the physical hosts will likely be the first thing you support in your career. We also focus on the MTA network certifications with group focus on cloud labs: Server 2016, Linux, and AWS.

Additionally, we employ Cisco Network Academy for students to use Packet tracer as a test or pre req for the class. Packet Tracer is a network simulation tool that is used to study for the Cisco CCENT or CCNA. It is a great free resource for those on the network engineering path.

Over 40+ people now have landed employment through my process. After obtaining the MTA certification, some of my students got hired at large enterprises with little experience. I know how to provide you with the direction and path to gain foundational experience and craft a standing resume. I know how to give you interview skills and point you in the right direction with resources. If you are willing to learn, I can help you be successful.

One thing I have to point out is that success often requires a leap of faith. For anyone that is interested in getting started in IT, you must be willing to accept the fact that you may have to take a pay cut and a contract role to get in. Sadly, some are not willing to do that. But look at it from the perspective of a recruiting agency that is taking the risk on you.

You are someone who barely knows anything about IT at this point or who is just getting started. They are not willing to risk putting you in a mid-level position because you do not have the experience just yet nor the background, but an entry-level position is all you need to get your foot in the door. Remember the risk I took? I was willing to give up my apartment to open the Minnehaha One Stop Shop with my friends. My rent was due, but I was convinced that we would have success and was determined to make it happen! You have to be willing to take 2 steps back to take 10 steps forward. That is not to say that you have to become poor to move up, but you have to let go of your fear of failure and get out of your comfort zone.

Had I stayed in my comfort zone and been afraid to fail, who knows where I would be now, but it would probably not look as good as it does now. With my music dream, I had no plan. But with IT, I had a plan. When I was working at Sears (which sucked), I told myself that I was better than $9 per hour. I wanted to quit so bad, but I said "I'ma work this punk-ass job until I cannot take it and use this dislike for it to push myself to get in something I do like." And then I set out for it. I achieved my goal—which was finding an IT training program—within 4 months (thanks to the Urban League). Another 6 months later, my friends and I opened a store on 38th and Nicollet. A few months later, I landed at a non-profit. A year later, I landed my first enterprise contract. Another year later, I opened another store. Every move I made fit into my plan. When you have a vision for yourself and your career, you can make anything happen.

Part 2: Your Guide to the IT Game

Most people think you have to be smart to be in IT, but you just have to know how to talk the talk and how to deliver. These are machines. God did not make them. We did. We are flawed, so we make flawed products. Flaws mean problems, and problems mean money for the people that can solve them (meaning us).

There was an article that recently came out that said something along the lines of "all motherboards from 2000 to now have vulnerability holes in them." That's a job for you! There are 1.7 million unfilled jobs in cyber security as it is. Also, regardless of how you feel about it, consider this: if the Commander in Chief is saying "America First," and they are cutting visas, what does that mean for you? Less competition.

I've told you a little bit about my story, and now I want to help you craft your own story. You have probably been told somewhere down the line that you must obtain a degree to even have a chance in the IT industry. I started in IT in 2007. It's 2019, and I still have yet to obtain a degree. You can do anything you want with hard work and dedication. The catch is that you have to be willing to work hard and to spend a lot of time teaching yourself new skills and technologies. With those things, you don't need a degree because you can prove your worth. I did it without a degree, and I'm going to give you a guide to do the same.

Before you read any further, I want you to stop and start writing your plan for your career. If you don't know what your goals are or where you see yourself in five years, this guide is not going to help you as much as it should. Everything I did, I wrote it down and constantly checked back each week to see if any tasks had been completed. A plan is only as good as its execution, so make sure you have a clear plan with checkpoints and tasks for you to accomplish along the way. Make a very detailed one-year plan and a general plan for the four years that follow.

Should I Go To College?

Colleges can provide a wealth of information (if you select a good college with great professors and a solid curriculum). The thing about college, though, is that it is slow and expensive.

When you enroll in college for a degree, you are in that program between two and four years. During that time, the technology you have learned about has already changed. Additionally, once you complete your degree, you won't have any experience to market yourself with unless you have actively sought internships, volunteer work, or otherwise worked in the industry while you obtained your degree. Once you graduate, that degree ain't gone make you $55K off the rip. I've seen college grads accept jobs at $12 per hour. The lucky ones might end up making $45K. But remember that you are $20-40K (if not more in some cases) in the hole thanks to your college education. You now have to work the next few years or so to pay off those loans; that's slavery. That should be a down payment for property or money to start a business.

So, if I enroll a student in my class who obtains a certification in two months and lands a role in another month, who is more efficient? I believe the days of brick and mortar education slave contracts will come to an end, and I have made it a personal goal of mine to help people avoid this abyss of anguish and financial ruin.

If you are in college, get certifications while you're there so that you are even more valuable once you complete your degree. Also, do some labs and put them on your resume.

If you are not in college, get your certifications, get hired on by a good company that offers tuition reimbursement, and let them pay for your college education.

Getting Started

I had the luxury of creating my own level 1 because my first tech jobs were in "field support." Remember, I started off hustlin in the streets. People already knew me, so I just had to reorganize my game plan and say "Hey, I do computers now!" It was an easy transition, and that was work experience that is considered field support. Don't downplay the experience you have.

When you start a new job in IT, just assume that the training will be subpar. This is why it is so important that you prepare and train yourself. If you can, build your own server with 16-24 GB of ram, an SSD drive for the OS, and a 4TB drive for storage or an NAS. Then slap a quad-core I5 in there or a nice AMD. A Lot of these companies do not want to train on working knowledge of the software, so in the words of the great Du'An Lightfoot, "Lab Everyday." Self-train as much as possible so that you can try and test multiple VMs. Take snapshots and break things. Invite a friend over to help, and use them as a lab rat and have them take notes. Buy a few brews, and turn it into a hangout. Hell, they may even become interested and become your IT improvement partner.

Know Your Goals and Values

In big enterprise, the CEOs and big wigs are less concerned with how you resolve a problem. They just care about the resolution. This is important because different teams handle this fact in different ways, and you need to determine what is important to you. Are you more into metric results or actual results? In other words, do you want to fix problems by a metric, or do you want to solve problems by root cause analysis? Metrics help close tickets, but they don't necessarily solve the full problem. You may get 10 more tickets just like that one, and if you don't solve the root cause, those tickets will keep appearing. It's a daily rat race of "nothing was truly fixed."

I never compromise my values for any job, but that is just me. Some people see no issue with solving problems by metrics, but that is not for me. I previously worked on a metrics-driven team that focused on churning out completed tickets and moving on to the next one. There came a point that I said, "No, I'ma fix this," and I almost got written up. They didn't want to fix it. They just wanted to keep churning those tickets and send it to level 2 or 3. I packed my bags and left. I made sure my next employer supported root-cause analysis.

Contracting

Contracting is a great way to get experience, and they usually pay well (and weekly). However, there are a few things you should be aware of when it comes to contracting.

Contracting firms make their money by charging their clients more than what they pay you. For instance, they might pay you $17 per hour and bill the client for $40 per hour. They won't tell how much they're charging the client, and they won't even tell you that there is a difference. This is good to be aware of because you can (and should) negotiate your pay.

Also, a lot of companies will tell you that a contract is temp to hire, but that really all depends. Companies may be paying a large hourly rate to the contracting firm for contractors, but it is cheaper to find Joe Smoe Recruiting, LLC to hire you as a contractor because they don't have to pay you benefits, contribute to your 401(k), or cover your insurance. And if you don't work out, they can just find another number.

As a contractor, you sometimes get stuck with crap work that the full-time IT pros do not want to do. I actually had a guy try to hand me a broom and mop. I just looked at him and smirked. No disrespect, but they have janitors for that, and I was not one of them. This is the extreme side, but just be aware that you may not be doing the most glamorous IT work.

Use contracts to your advantage to make good money, gain experience, and keep it pushing. Test the waters, and do not get discouraged. Get good enough that you are undeniable, and keep moving up.

Understand Job Descriptions

Do not expect the job description to match all of the duties. Job posts are just regurgitated descriptions that are reused over and over and are not updated. Do not assume that the job will be exactly as it is described in the job post because when you arrive, it could be completely different.

I was working at Cargill when I really started to understand how different the job listing can be compared to what you actually do every day. I was getting $37 per hour, and all I did was push apps on the EUC team and fly to different states to open Putty for Cisco engineers to desegregate their networks. Here is the job description for that job posting, and I bolded the items that I actually needed/used:

We are a national staffing firm and are currently seeking an EUC Desktop Engineer for a prominent client of ours. This position is located in Hopkins, MN. Details for the position are as follows:

5+ Years of experience on end-user computing.

- Knowledge of TCO for PC Imaging and application packaging as well as OS bundling
- Hands-on experience in Application packaging
- Comprehensive working knowledge on SCCM (System Center Configuration Manager) 2012 for application deployment
- Hands-on experience on Server level OS (Windows 2008, Win 2012) and desktop level OS (Win 7 and Win 8)
- Troubleshooting deployment issues

- Knowledge of DNS, DHCP, and VPN etc.
- Knowledge of Commvault back up agent (back up process)
- Knowledge of Software licensing
- Knowledge of printers and print management, desktop hardware
- Basic networking knowledge
- Knowledge of ITSM ticketing tools
- Good communication and articulation skills
- Group policies creation

Desirable to have

- Knowledge of powershell scripting
- Knowledge of Citrix technology
- Knowledge of VMWare

Notice that I never touched half the stuff in the job description. These Indian guys did the other work and helped me complete some of it. They covered me when I did not know certain things, and we made everything work as a team (Note that this is what our brothers and sisters must do with each other rather than always competing or hating).

Interview with Confidence

When you start looking for a job, treat looking for a job like it is a job itself. Apply for a minimum of five jobs per day. Some companies you should consider applying to are Travelers, TCS, and Blue Cross. I recommend Travelers to all new guys. If you can get on their Help Desk team, they are a great place to start. They don't bombard you with metrics, and they have mandatory breaks. TCS has good training, and they're almost as good as a government job—you will be there for years if you do your best. Blue Cross is good once you have some experience because they always have a ton of data and BA roles. There is a brother on YouTube called Angelo the BA, and he has some insightful content, so check him out.

As you get more certifications and feel more confident in your skills, interviewing will get easier and easier. In the beginning, you will be more nervous because you're trying to convince someone that you have what they need for that position with little to back you up. But eventually, your certifications and experience will do most of the talking for you.

Until then, ensure that you have a strong understanding of foundational network skills. You should have basic working knowledge of Wireshark or another network analyzer, and you should also understand DHCP, DNS, Domains, and protocols. You should know about Server 2008-2016 and about the new technologies and trends.

You should also know how to professionally communicate through email as well as bridge/conference call etiquette. On a conference call, announce yourself and do not interrupt. Assume that mute button does not work!

Be familiar with tone and cadence, and have confidence when doing phone support. Listen to the caller explain the issue, then ask questions and dive in. Understand what it means to own a ticket and how to drive it into completion while including other notable coworkers when necessary.

Update your resume every time you learn a new skill or obtain a certification. Your resume does not need to be a bible; compress it, but make it interesting. You want to tell a quick, stand out story. And for the love of God, whatever you put on that resume, be ready to prove your understanding of it in an interview. Don't put anything on your resume that you can't explain when asked. Also, make a brief cover letter for each job that you apply to.

Once you get an interview, buy a thank you card to mail to the interviewer, and mail it as soon as your interview is over. During the interview, you should maintain eye contact and have three relevant and unique questions. In the past, I have even gone on to D & B Hoovers to find a company's financial growth and reports. I stunned that interviewer when I said "I noticed you generated a revenue of $10 million this year in sales. That's incredible. How were you able to pull that off?" The interviewers said, "Good question!" You got 'em then. "Good question" means "I don't have an answer," and they will fumble to find one. Then, I turn to the next person and ask them what they least like about their job. They really get stuck on that. No one wants to answer that question without making the company look bad. It works for me every time. And I always have answers and examples for question they ask me. There have been times where I did so well in an interview that they didn't offer me the job, but they gave me their colleague's number for another job lead.

Situation questions? Piece of cake. Mention any three conflicts you had that you resolved, and give a story. These questions are pre-written, and they are intended to make you stumble if you are not prepared. Put your interview suit on, and practice with a few friends by having them grill you. If you really want to boost your interview skills, have someone record it so they can nitpick your blunders to death. Replay the interview until you have it down.

I once had an interview where I was asked, "what is your favorite Sesame Street character." The question was a trick. It was not about me liking Sesame Street or some psycho-analysis of which character I selected. I could have said I liked Kermit the Frog because he is green and I like Frogs, but the question was testing my ability to think outside of the box. It was a company culture question. I answered with: "The Count. The count likes numbers. Numbers are informational and empirical. Also, the Count is a vampire. He is based off Count Dracula, and that tale was based off Vlad the Impaler. They actually had a movie based off of his true character called Dracula Untold, but they did not cover the fact that he was raised in a Turkish home." They hired me.

Dress as you want to be perceived. Treat it like you would treat a date. If you were going on a date, would you go dirty? If so, you may want to stay at home. Don't even waste their time. As my Mom, would say, "Come right or don't come at all! You must have some type of respect for yourself when you leave the door." Even the red light district workers have some dignity. You need to dress the part.

Coming new into the game, you have less pull. But once you get more experience, you'll be able to be more choosy about finding the best fit for you. I once had an interview where the receptionist rudely blurted out that getting me coffee was complicated. That already let me know what that company's culture was like, and I passed up on that job. It just didn't feel right. They kept their $70K, but I had the luxury to say no and move on. Any time I apply for a job, I want to know what kind of commute I'll have, how much it will cost me in gas, whether I like the side of town they're in, all that. You'll learn when a good-sounding offer is really garbage in disguise.

When you ask the interviewer your questions, you may also consider asking what their company culture is like, if they offer work from home opportunities, if there is room for growth, if they offer performance or referral incentives, and if they pay for certifications.

Most importantly, say "I am an asset" 3 times before you leave your car to go into an interview, and believe it. You are worthy of any job they have to offer; you just have to sell it.

Know Your Monetary Worth

Here is a glimpse of the pay you can expect for certain IT jobs:

Help Desk: $12-20 p/hr.
Desktop: $20-25 p/hr.
Cyber Security: $30-40 p/hr.
BA/Data analyst: $62-100K salary

As a newbie in the industry, you will probably make between $12 and $17 per hour. The money will come through your certifications, such as the MTA and the Cisco CCNA Cyber Ops. Salesforce has some free training called Trailhead that you should look into. Salesforce is a CRM system that many large and medium companies use to manage, track, and monetize. Those that can administer it can become a dangerous resource, commanding a good pay rate. Go to https://trailhead.salesforce.com/ and take the beginning admin courses. It allows you to setup a sandbox and test it. This is good experience for a prospective role, and Salesforce is a prime place to get out of the cumbersome help desk and graveyard support realm. When you support the Salesforce environment, users cannot bully you into a resolution; they must wait for a change or upgrade. If the software has a bug, Salesforce itself has to fix it. You have the freedom to learn as you go without the high expectations or stress of a call center. The Salesforce community is large and giving, like the Linux community, with plenty of resources. It's about making the environment better, so there are fewer burnouts. You get a Salesforce certification, and you are the man (or the woman)!

You may start to eventually notice that half of these companies hire H1B Visa candidates so that they don't have to pay us locals the fair price. For example, I knew a guy from India who was a CCNP—a very senior network/security architect. He asked me how much I was making. I don't usually like talking about my pay with coworkers, but he was a big dog, and all he could do was help me. I told him I was making $37 per hour, and he told me he was making $25. I almost fainted. This guy was doing $125K worth of work for $25 per hour. But he was not a US citizen. He had to take the sharecrop deal and stay on the plantation. If he complained, they would ship him back to India as easily as a returned Amazon gift. I reached out to a few recruiters I knew and told them I knew a Senior CCNP Cisco engineer that needed a sponsorship to work. I found him a few places, and he ended up in San Jose. (This is another example of why networking is valuable. Always use opportunities to connect with other people.)

That company tried to play me too. They wanted me to work for 2 weeks for free. I told them to go to hell and said I would be calling the Department of Labor. I got a call from the recruiter within 15 minutes begging me to not to call. These jokers had a $2,500 check in my account within 24 hours. Don't let anyone play you! The day you have a company force you to work for free may be the last day you ever have to work again. If you are not salary, an employer is committing a crime asking you to work without pay.

Some IT professionals are treated like trash. We used to be valued, but due to automation, some places only provide an insultingly low level of pay. This is why you should not stay in support. Help desk work should not be long term. Use these positions in the beginning of your career to get experience, and then move on and up. Consider data roles and business analyst positions because that is where the money is at.

The days of staying stagnant at one company as an IT professional for 40 years are over. Technology changes like fake friends. Every 6 months, there is something new. Azure and AWS is now taking us by storm. These companies have to pay you for your experience and your knowledge, but you are only worth what you can show for yourself. If you are well-versed in server, cloud, and Python platforms, you can pretty much name your price. The effort you put into your career and self-training will result in your check amount.

When it comes to salary for a permanent position, you want the complete package: 401(k), health, dental, vision, and good PTO. So, if you get offered $55K, just know that is with everything included. It is not $55K, plus benefits (in many cases). Make them break down what they are actually paying you before you sign anything.

Learn How to Negotiate

One of the best skills I learned as a contractor was how to negotiate with recruiters. Most of them know nothing about technology. They can type and talk, and their job is to determine if you are a good fit for the contract based on what the client has written down on paper. Reassure them of your skills and experience, and don't let them talk you out of a job that you know you can do. I have met guys that knew nothing and still managed to get into some of those positions. It is all about how you market yourself.

As I said, I don't like to discuss pay, but I want to be very honest and give you a glimpse into how my pay has changed over the years:

2007: Desktop Support for Urban Ventures Internship: $10 p/hr.
2008: Desktop Support for Coloplast Corp: $16 p/hr.
2010: Apple Support/Tech Analyst for Connex: $17 p/hr.
2012: Windows 7 Specialist for Minco: $17 p/hr.
2013: Windows 7 Specialist for Blue Cross: $19 p/hr.
2013: Desktop Analyst III for Travelers: $25 p/hr.
2014: Desktop Support for Medica: $25 p/hr.
2014: Windows 7 Team Lead/Reporting Analyst for AIG: $25 p/hr.
2015: EUC Engineer for TCS: $37 p/hr.

And my pay has continued to increase every year since then. Notice the lateral growth. I kept teaching myself new skills, and my positions and pay reflect that. You should be changing your job every two years. You can stay at the same company, but you should be expanding and diversifying your work portfolio and volunteering to learn new lines of business and technologies. We all know a guy that has been at a company for 15 years and stayed in the exact same position. You would think another company would love this experience and loyalty, but that is not always the case. Many companies will say that he is too stagnant and that they "can't teach an old dog new tricks." Companies like ambitious and energetic people who know how to push the envelope without causing a wrinkle.

Land a 6 month or so contract and if that does not extend, go to the next. When the recruiters ask about your previous pay, say I want $20-25 per hour. I have had recruiters call about the same job from 10 different recruitment companies. If one won't negotiate with you, another one will.

Be Smart With Your Money

In the black community, we learn a lot of bad money habits and aren't taught about how to make money off of the white collar system. I'm from the generation where you were judged based on the size of your rims, the paint on your old school ride, and your attire. Your goal was to command respect on the street by your material goods. This is the socially engineered culture that provoked a lack of true wealth management and acquisition amongst the black population, in my opinion. I've known and seen hustlers make a ton of money on the streets and just blow it on Jordans and whips. Imagine if there was a Black Wall Street where they could all put their money together to make even more money and better the community.

If I knew about 401(k)s and investments in my early years, I could have had at least $150K by now. You want to start thinking about 401(k)s, mutual funds, and stock investments. Being just a consumer should be temporary.

One big mistake I made was staying in an apartment complex for 8 years. I left owning nothing. An older guy had told me, "Derek, you are in a frozen state of independence. You are grown and live on your own, but you are building someone else's dream. You have nothing to show for your hard work except that you can you say you are a grown man with cars and clothes." This struck a nerve for me because I knew it was true. I gave those apartment people 8 years of my life and salary just to say I was independent. Imagine if I would have stayed at home a little longer and saved that money instead. I would have had a down payment on land. Moral of the story, don't spend your life in an apartment. Start saving up for a home you can own as soon as possible.

Another smart money decision is not purchasing a new car. Avoid car payments at all cost in the beginning of your career. If you purchase an older vehicle, always keep at least $500 to the side in case it needs repairs. You want to be seen as a reliable asset, and being late due to beaters is not cool, nor a good look.

Look at your ride as an investment to work. It's a tool, not a flex. Once you've been working for a while and have steady income, put a down payment on something affordable and reliable, and keep the car you own until the financed one is paid off. If your new car needs repairs, you can always use the old car. Plus, you may have a repo. I pray this doesn't happen to you, but it happened to me, so I just have to keep it real. Always ensure that you are able to get to work no matter what.

Another smart way to handle your money is by properly filing your taxes. If you are doing side hustles or working 1099, Intuit is a great app that helps you deduct your mileage, materials, and anything else you've used/purchased for business in the course of the year. I track any and everything. When I instruct my classes, I count that gas and mileage. If I purchase a new laptop, it is a business expense. Recording a podcast at the studio was an expense. My certification for Microsoft or Citrix was an expense. The coffee for business meetings was an expense. GoToMeeting or any software-as-a service you may use each month is an expense. Anything you do that is in regards to your business and is legally taxable is an expense. This is how your top politicians and people who own software companies stay afloat.

Networking

I recommend attending conferences, webinars, meetups, and forums. The BDPA, Blacks in IT, and the Urban League often have programs. Instead of wasting all of your free time watching Power, Housewives, or meaningless YouTube videos, you should dedicate the same amount of time to learning a new tool and honing your skills. Those meaningless shows will not improve your skills or increase your pay. You can still enjoy television, but be sure to spend time investing in yourself as well.

Join a few technical Meetup groups (Splunk, Appdynamics, Powershell, Cybersec, and many more) and actually attend some of the meetings. The more people that you meet, the more people that are in your network. Being organic is key. I strike convo with anyone that has a kindred spirit. That's how I've made money. You should present yourself like each encounter could be an interview. Get that haircut. Wear nice shoes. Pop a mint in your mouth. I almost landed a job at a Splunk conference just from talking to a guy who was also attending. I was not looking for work, but my approach and presentation impressed him enough to want to hire me.

When you go out to network, make sure you have business cards to market yourself with. Haystack is a great app that lets you design your own business card and pass it out digitally. When I network with people, they usually wait for me to reach for my wallet to give them a card until I say, "I'll send you my digital card." Then they're amazed. My blog is also on my card, so it allows me to promote my website and my book. Market yourself in a memorable way so that you stay at the top of their minds.

Schmooze 'Em

Do you share small details about your personal life? Did you shrug off an incident of disrespect? Did you attend all the company outings and happy hours? This "ass kissing" can truly determine the outcome of your career. You would think that your quality of work would be enough to get you to the top, but if you want those senior, high paying careers, it's not. The work is 40 percent. The schmoozing is 60 percent. When you go to apply for a promotion and you haven't made an effort to make yourself known and liked among the group, they're going to be thinking "Jerome is not a team player" or "Jerome just doesn't seem to fit in with our company culture." They're not going to be thinking about why you didn't attend any of the outings; they're just going to remember that you weren't there.

I saw this play out with one of my coworkers. He did not come to an afterwork party, and he was ridiculed for it. I watched in disgust as these guys tore into this man without him even being there.

In the corporate world, you need allies. You need people that like you and can vouch for you if you ever needed them to. But be mindful of who you ally with because they may not actually have your back the way they pretend that they do. Share small details about your life that make people feel like they know you (things you like to do, hobbies, your spouse, kids), but don't overshare. Don't talk about your finances, major purchases, drama, or anything you wouldn't want thrown back in your face later.

References

I had a few colleagues that were conflicted about moving on to a better opportunity because they were worried about references. I am here to dispel the myths of references. Dates and titles are all you need. Most companies will only confirm that information anyway. Legally, when a company calls to verify employment, the previous employer can only verify that you worked there. They cannot say anything negative about your character or about your work ethic. Don't get me wrong, references can still be incredibly valuable, but you can always find a character reference from a coworker.

If you are attending college or a technical school, they can also provide references. You are paying them thousands of dollars, so understand that you should get everything you need from them, including references. If they refuse to provide you with a reference and you have good grades, contact the dean to find ways to get references. They might even end up providing you a reference themself.

Coworkers

Throughout your career, regardless of what your role is or where you work, you will work with people that you like and with some that you don't. It is important that you understand how to communicate effectively and professionally with your coworkers regardless of how you feel about them, however.

Don't expect your black coworkers to automatically have your back just because you're both black. Honestly, sometimes the black ones can be the worst ones, especially if they were originally the token black guy before you got there. I worked with a brother that went out of his way to watch my every move and try to catch me slippin. I pulled him to the side and asked him if they paid him more for trying to get me in trouble. He told me they did not. If he was going to act like a secret agent around there, he should have at least been getting paid for that extra work. But for him, it was all about social acceptance. People would rather have clout than anything, and I could not respect that. It wasn't like he was going to get a lead position by trying to get me out the way. I ended up at a managed services company doing Citrix support. So, jokes on him. A lot of times, when building solidarity with a brother or sister at work, if they express their opinion on a matter, I'll agree with "Fa-sho" just to test their reaction. If they look funny at me, then I know that they just want to be socially accepted and are put off by my display of "blackness" at work, even if it was just between the two of us. They are willing to fake it at every turn just to fit in—they won't take any chances of appearing "too black," which means that they will likely backstab me any chance they get to prove their loyalty to everyone else (especially if we are the only blacks in there, which is typical).

Read body language, because what people say is not what they always mean. Be mindful and watchful.

If a manager or supervisor talks to you about something they say you did wrong or something you need to do differently in the future, just take it as a verbal warning—whether they said it is one or not. Don't let them tell you something more than once.

Because new hires are often labeled as "do nothings," I used to document all of my daily actions and training. Call me paranoid, but I have had people take credit for my deployments and then turn right around and say that my work did not get done. Do what you have to do to make sure that no one can throw you under the bus. Sometimes you may have the "first day" harassers. These folks are not your manager, but they feel the need to be an overseer of your work. Ignore them and tell them you are still training. One guy asked me how I landed a permanent job. He made it seem like I was not supposed to have it. He asked me if I was proud to be there. I almost told him if I owned it I would be proud. I guess he thought that job was the best I was going to get. Meanwhile, he never made it past help desk.

I will tell you what an Azure architect shared with me: "We, as minorities, have to be on top of our game. Look through the jobs, see the qualifications, and master them all. Never let your color determine your genius." But we are not minorities. You are major, not minor. Think like a king and treat others like royalty.

Shake Them Haters Off

When you're doing well, especially when you're doing better than the people around you, there will be haters. There will be people who wish your success was theirs but either don't know how or are too lazy to make it happen for themselves. They will try to block your shine.

For example, a friend of mine was working as an intern for a company in Coon Rapids, Minnesota. She got her A.A.S. degree in networking and also earned a Cisco CCNA. The network admin at her job tried to keep her from moving up, but she landed the certification and applied some of her cable management skills on the routers and switches in the network closet. The network admin was upset about that. The truth was, he could not pass his CCNA, and he had been at the company for years. He also was angry that a woman of color had more skills within a year than he had within 15 years.

You may have people at your job that do not want you to succeed, but be undeniable. Let them hate while you focus on becoming a SME.

Harassment at Work

You should not involve yourself in chatty patty conversations or participate in workplace gossip of any shape or form. You are there to grow your career and get the bag!

There will always be one person that gives you a particularly hard time, and the best way to deal with them is by keeping your distance. Keep your conversations at work strictly about work. Don't start discussing racism, politics, or anything else that can get a debate started. If someone is racist towards you, let them be that. Write their comments down and get them canned! Lawyer up, if necessary. We have to start doing the Roseanne with these folks. You do your job and keep your mouth shut. If they want to burn a cross in their backyard at home, fine. But when those actions put their jobs at stake, they will learn then.

Any time something negative happens at work, document it. Even if you think it will never happen again. If someone is harassing you at work, take notes. Dates, times, names. In the streets, I honored handshake deals, but in the corporate world, talk means nothing if it isn't written down. Paper trails are how people win cases and how tyrants fall. If you have issues of harassment, skip over your manager and go to HR.

If the situation is bad enough that it is beyond HR, go to the Department of Labor or the EOC. Only write to the Department of Labor if there is an issue and you have very strong evidence to support it. For instance, if you get canned from a company and you feel you were done wrong. After you've been fired, submit a written request (email) to the employer within 7 days of your termination. If you don't receive a response, show this request to the Department of Labor, and the employer will be required to provide the Department of Labor with a response within 30 days or they can be fined. Minnesota is an at-will state, which means that they can fire you for any reason. But if they do, they have to report to the Department of Labor fairly, by law. No matter what the situation is, make sure you have paperwork to prove anything your claim, and never lie about what occurred.

If you get canned, regardless of whatever reason, get back to self-training. This is the time that you use to focus on landing a certification or studying to get acclimated to other technologies. This is not the time for Netflix to be your main course. If you were fired or laid off at no fault of your own, you must be paid unemployment. This is your money—never let anyone convince you otherwise because you worked and paid into your employer's insurance. The money won't be enough to get comfy, but it is enough to support you while you go down to the state office and ask what IT certification funding they have so you can train and land a new job. If you are fired from a job you were at many years, look at this transition as an opportunity to move up in your career.

Minnesota can't retain a lot of tech workers because discrimination is still thick here, even though they try to hide it. They have mastered microaggressions; they may pass you up for an upper management position only to hire someone less qualified or find ways to take small jabs at you. For example, I have been in meetings where I expressed my opinion and no one wanted to hear what I had to say. But then if I got quiet, I was told that I was not contributing to the conversation. These lose-lose situations are common because they can get away with it. You may have someone say you are slacking off while they sip coffee and gossip in the break room for 30 minutes.

Another example: I spoke with a brother that was working as an IT director at a Fortune 500 company in Downtown Mpls. Even at that level, he said that when he sits in meetings, they act like he shouldn't be there. They even asked him what he was doing there one time. Another brother in Stillwater found a noose in his toolbox. He tried to get help and was basically told to get over it. The problem with a lot of these scenarios that you might find yourself in is that you cannot prove it.

I had to report a few fools myself before they got the message. Thing is, my plan was tight. If the environment gets too bad, be on your way out the door. Don't suffer stress and bad health over a check—you are an asset! But like a frog, make sure you have another lily pad in close distance before you hop off the one you have. Don't land in the pond. Secure yourself. I'm going to keep telling you about certifications because they are important. Study the materials, get certified, and become a SME. Leave your emotions at home, and do not engage in negativity. Put good energy out into the universe, and you will get it right back.

Here's a story for you: I was working at a firm downtown (which I won't name). My performance review was good, and I was resolving the majority of the team's tickets each week. I was told at hiring that I would have 6 months of training in this very complex Citrix environment. Well, within 2 months I was training the offshore team and my manager tried to help sabotage me by telling the team to withhold information from me. Then she tried to set up a meeting to blame me for completing duties as I was trained and instructed to do. While she was trying to build a case against me, I found a data position and put in my 2 weeks. She tried to put me in a bad position and the only one left in a bad position was her. The team had already lost 3 citrix guys with 3 more to be leaving soon. That manager was in the process of being removed from her position because as she was not doing a good job integrating the team. Her plan was to use me as a scapegoat by pinning all the deployment failures on me- and many of those failures were due to her telling the team to refuse to provide information on processes and tools. Gotta love that karma. The day I announced my resignation, I copied HR and my manager on a scathing email that listed the reasons for my resignation.

If you live in Minnesota or a state with similar disparities, consider earning your experience and certifications and making that migration back to the South where there is more diversity and where you will be more appreciated. Mpls is beautiful city. It is my home. But it has a dark and cold history when it comes to keeping a microaggressive ceiling for people that look like us. This is even more of a reason that we should be more supportive of each other and be willing to share new opportunities to grow economically. If we don't help each other, no one else will.

Put Your Health First

Sometimes you have to hold back some of your energy for yourself; otherwise people might try to use you to their advantage. You want to be compensated for your skillset and your time. I have seen good workers get overworked because they were more skilled. You don't want to be doing $80K worth of work for a $65K salary. Some would argue with me, but your health is more important than that company.

So, here is what you can do: slow the work down a bit—you don't have to be the fastest worker there. When you fly through work (and you do it correctly), the company isn't going to just let you sit around and do nothing. No, they are going to try to give you more work to do. Divide your work, mark it down on calendars, and communicate via email for documentation.

Jobs should not harm your heart. You are there to perform a business transaction that should benefit both parties. It's not a sound business deal if you are being mistreated and are stressed. If you are going to the doctor because of work, fire your boss! Life is short. Leave. You can vent to your loved ones, but don't complain if you have no plan to change it. Vent and write down a viable plan for a way out.

Sometimes you might even have to walk away from what seemed like an amazing opportunity. For example, a friend of mine landed his dream job at an antivirus company in Roseville, MN. He was hired as a software support engineer, and things were immediately off to a horrible start. The company didn't have a good communication system in place, and their training was subpar. By the time he made it through the "training program," he still didn't have the tools he needed to be successful on the phones. Meanwhile, the new hires made racist jokes and comments that had nothing to do with work. My friend ended up going to the doctor from the stress of the job. Don't let any job get you to that point.

Before making a move, ask yourself: Is my bag right? Can I afford to fire my boss? Is my job causing bad health? Will leaving help me grow? How will it affect my family? If you determine that you are stable enough and that it is worth it, secure yourself and leave.

If you plan to leave but aren't able to yet, stack your bag and tell no one of your plan. In the meantime, find something outside of work to hold on to: family, hobbies, religion, anything. Do some mediation and self-study. See if you can switch positions at the same company.

Give yourself 1-3 months (or more) to find a new gig. The best time to look for work is the first quarter, and the worst time is the fourth quarter. Keep in mind that you will always be in a better position if you look for a job while you still have one. There was a time when I looked for a new position for one year and turned down four interviews and four offers before I found something I wanted. Because I still had a job, I could afford to be picky.

Don't ever feel bad about moving on from a job. They can put their balloons on your desk and say they don't know what they'll do without you, but you are moving on because God has other plans for you. You have other plans for you. They will find someone else. And you don't have to have a tirade and act a fool when you leave. Be professional. Shake a few hands, and celebrate.

If you end up with gaps on your resume, you should volunteer and obtain certifications and put that on your resume. That is no gap! Explain that you have been training. There are webinars and classes that count as CPE credits. CPE credit conferences, online courses, or anything technical counts towards continuing education. Programs will tell you if they are CPE eligible, and some of them are free. Some IT certifications will require that you attend something so that you to stay hip to what is going on in the industry.

In the end, make the best decision for your finances and your mental health. If you are determined, you can make any situation work to your benefit.

Software and Technology Recommendations

Some of the tools I recommend for you to start using and learning include:

Active Directory
AWS
Azure
Bomgar
Google Cloud
Haystack (for digital business cards)
Microsoft Office, especially Excel
PfSense
Power BI
Powershell
Putty
Python
Server 2012 R2
Server 2016
Server 2019
Tableau
Teamviewer
Ubuntu (or Kali Linux)
VmWare
Windows 10 version 1809
Wireshark

A lot of this software has free trials. If you are in school, you can get licenses at no cost or for a reduced fee. You want to become familiar with any and all technology that you can.

Active directory is like a big phone book of who can do what. Invite a few buddies over and deny and grant them access to their accounts. Learn it well.

Citrix takes a good 1-2 years to be able to understand because there are so many moving parts. If you are able to get into an environment where you are able to touch some of the tools that will help you learn Citrix, that would be helpful (though it isn't super likely if you don't have much experience). Practice in server administration is key, networking is essential, and an SSL certificate or PKI understanding is good too. Citrix sits on servers, so the more you know about AD, DNS, and virtualization, the better. A lot of companies want to get away from Citrix because of the cloud, but there will be companies using Citrix for at least 5-10 more years, if not more.

Read up on Citrix products such as Receiver (now Workspace), Xencenter, Netscaler, Xenapp, and XenDesktop. Positions that support this technology can make you $55K on your first go round.

Certifications

Take the 77-272 exam and get the Excel certification. Then, knock out that 98-366 MTA certification (there are even practice tests online for it). All of my students aim to land this certification. Networking is the building block of being successful in this industry. You will gain the exposure you need to have a sound convo in an interview with this exam. It also exposes you to other necessary concepts. These exams will suffice for most going into data and BA positions.

A Perfect World Plan

If I could plan out your career for you (and it was a perfect world where it would happen exactly as I planned it), your plan would go something like this:

Start your career with internships or volunteer work. People value someone who will offer a helping hand, just don't get taken advantage of. You need to be paid something for your experience whether it is in money, valuable connections/networking, or experience with a new tool that you can slap on your resume.

Get a contract at a large enterprise in a help desk role. You will take calls, reset passwords, and answer questions for people that act like they just upgraded from a typewriter yesterday. Expect to have some understanding of Active Directory, Windows 10, and IOS/Android phones. If you have some call center experience, you are in there. To prepare yourself for your next role, learn imaging. Set up your own Windows deployment lab to get the concepts down. Use Server 2012 or 2016, and get the WDS deployment tool running with Windows 10. This way, you will be able to deploy a Windows OS. You can find this on YouTube (hell, I'll send you some info if you email me). The nice thing about building your own virtualized deployment lab is that you can control what you deploy. You have a domain controller, a WDS server, and your client VM. You will need at least 16-32 GB of memory with a i5 or i7. Allow 8GB or less for your domain controller, 4GB for WDS server and another 4GB for the client. Use Hyper V or VmWare workstation.

After a while, move into Level 2 or desktop support at a medium-sized company and work on becoming a SME. You'll make $14 to $17 per hour your first go. After that, shoot for $20 for the next role. For those who enjoy working more with hardware than dealing with support calls, you may be able to land a desktop role first. Many of you will enjoy this more because you will be imaging machines and perhaps working with more hardware. You could be adding network printers and accessories or peripherals like monitors and scanners. Some support will be face-to-face. Desktop positions usually head toward the server path, so keep that in mind.

Another thing to know and understand is the difference between the private and public sector. Private sector is usually for money-making or service-selling companies, and they offer better pay but often have more politics. All of the problems I've listed that I or someone I knew had at work with office politics occurred at a company in the private sector. Non-profit companies are usually in the public sector. This includes schools and community organizations. They often don't pay as well as the private sector, but the culture is often made of smaller teams that are more family oriented, the people are more focused and motivated, and the work is meaningful. They have to be more creative with their infrastructure and spending because they don't have money to blow like the big dogs do, and sometimes the organization can get as gossipy as a small town, but the culture is typically the best selling point of non-profit work. Plus, these jobs often come with good benefits, there is rarely weekend work, you can sometimes get cheap park and ride passes through the county or state, and you will have a long-term career that might even allow you to move around.

Back to the plan—if you have gained exposure to vmware and

servers at this point, you can officially ask for $50K+ if you've still been getting your one certification or so a year. You can now prove your experience with documentation. If you plan to become a system admin, you will need to know about servers and imaging, and a scripting language helps too. With your experience, you might be able to work for a managed services provider (MSP). MSP companies basically provide IT support for other companies; instead of those companies having their own IT staff, you are the staff. They're are usually small companies, however, and people don't leave often, so these positions are harder to come by. But if you can get on, you can ask for $57K and above.

Become a business analyst or a data analyst. This is where the money is at.

Conclusion

Look at my path. I started out in the hood selling mixtapes, socks, and t-shirts, started doing home PC repair, landed an internship, landed multiple enterprise migration contracts, and became a Citrix administrator. Then I started training brothers and sisters in the same streets I roamed around in—mentoring them and helping them land Microsoft certifications and gainful employment. My journey has been far from flawless, but I have lived a rewarding life, and I feel like I am doing rewarding work. It feels good to be able to say you helped change someone's life. I plan for my next path to be to train other instructors to duplicate my curriculum so that we can help even more of our people.

Before it is said and done, IT and medical will be the last fields left. Get in while the getting is good. Get certified. Gain the knowledge. Make your own lane.

For questions about this book, my classes, resume services, or for booking inquiries, email me at derek@beingblackinIT.com or go to www.beingblackinIT.com to order products and services.

About the Author

Derek Pearson was born in Minneapolis, Minnesota in 1982. He started in the Information Technology field in 2008 working at various enterprises and non-profits to support their infrastructure. Derek also managed retail stores for computer sales and repair. He attended Century College where he received an Associate of Arts degree in 2019 after 10 years in the IT world with no formal education. He now lives in Saint Paul, MN as a data analyst and technical trainer for the tech community of the Twin Cities, where he offers employment and IT certification assistance.

Learn more about Derek and his services by visiting www.beingblackinIT.com.

76034005R00045

Made in the USA
Columbia, SC
22 September 2019